Peter Herring and Peter Rose

one and all *onen hag oll*
CORNWALL
COUNTY COUNCIL

Cornwall Archaeological Unit

This booklet is a general introduction to the landscape history and extremely important archaeological remains of Bodmin Moor in east Cornwall. It has been prepared by the Cornwall Archaeological Unit.

Material gathered from detailed surveys undertaken over the past 20 years has formed the basis of the text so the area covered is largely confined to the granite uplands. It does not extend into those lowlands around Bodmin Moor which are also included in the Bodmin Moor Project area. The booklet is not a guide to sites, but is instead an introduction to the types of archaeological remains found on the Moor; its principal aim is to help owners and those with an interest to understand the meaning and importance of the remains. Archaeological sites on Bodmin Moor are on private land, and permission to visit must be obtained from owners and, where appropriate, Commoners' Associations.

Contents

Introduction

Bodmin Moor, the largest of the Cornish granite uplands, has a wealth of archaeological remains that few parts of Britain can equal. In prehistory the uplands were used with a surprising intensity, reflecting the value of these wide tracts of rough pasture to a people whose beliefs and ideas are tantalisingly displayed in their stone circles and stone rows, their barrows and cairns. Their fields and settlements of round-houses remain a testimony to a way of life remote from our own. The quality of preservation is such that one can still pass between prehistoric gateposts to walk down a trackway through prehistoric fields, along to the circular farmhouse itself with its collapsed walling and fallen doorposts. What is especially valuable is the survival of whole blocks of prehistoric landscape, with repeating patterns of settlements and fields. Next to them, apparently integral parts of the pattern, lie the ceremonial and ritual monuments. In this

Continuity and change on Sharp Tor's southern slopes. Overlapping field patterns confirm that this has been at the margin of cultivation since the establishment in prehistoric times of the curvilinear enclosures whose ploughed-over boundaries cast low shadows. The straighter shadowy line running across them is a later prehistoric pasture boundary. A sinuous medieval hedged lane crosses them all towards the left. Straight-sided fields linking the lane to the straight wall against the Moor are early modern.
© CAU/CCC

The Archaeological Heritage of Bodmin Moor

context even the stretches of open moorland apparently devoid of archaeological remains have meaning and value. These too were part of the prehistoric landscape, providing the extensive rough grazing that brought people onto the Moor in the first place. Tors, streams, marshes and other natural features will also probably have had meanings for prehistoric people.

In Cornwall it is only on Bodmin Moor that certain types of prehistoric monument survive in such diversity. Many types of site are virtually unknown elsewhere in the county and Bodmin Moor forms the major reservoir of potential information about many aspects of prehistoric Cornwall. We must remember that as there is, by definition, no historical documentation for the many millennia of 'prehistory', we depend entirely on the archaeological sites. These have subtle and complex layers below ground, as well as walls and earthworks above. They are fragile and irreplaceable documents.

For the medieval period, on the other hand, documentary evidence helps to set the deserted hamlets and fields into the context of manor and parish. They can be seen to belong to the same framework of farms and fields that prevails today. Swept up onto the Moor by the rising tide of an expanding medieval population in the 11th to 14th centuries, and abandoned with its ebbing, the farms and hamlets retain their layout intact. They have a pattern of ruined buildings, garden plots and trackways that simply has not survived elsewhere in Cornwall. Similarly it is only on Bodmin Moor that one can see the complete layout of medieval field systems, surviving as they were abandoned.

The windswept, virtually treeless granite upland, punctuated by craggy tors, is in contrast to the countryside that surrounds it. This is often lush and sheltered by comparison and interrupted by small wooded valleys cut by fast flowing streams. This too is an ancient landscape. Here, many of the present-day farms are on sites occupied since long before the Norman Conquest, and are linked by twisting sunken lanes that must be equally old. The woods, found particularly on the southern and eastern fringes, are fragments of woodland that was already ancient at the time of Domesday Book (1086).

These more favourable lowland fringes have seen continuous settlement since early in prehistory. This very continuity has, however, all but obliterated traces of prehistoric activity that would have been more intensive and more enduring than that on the uplands.

Contemporary with the medieval hamlets are many of the tin streamworks where valley bottoms, and some hillsides, have been systematically dug over to extract tin gravels. Historically Bodmin Moor, or 'Foweymore', was once Cornwall's most important medieval Stannary (tin producing area). Evidence for this early industry is best preserved here. Industry's influence was most powerful, of course, in the 19th century when tin and copper mining, together with quarrying and china-clay working, shook up the settlement and farming patterns: new hamlets grew; large tracts of unenclosed moorland were divided into farms and smallholdings and taken in by the hardworking families of farmers and labourers.

The south-east corner of Bodmin Moor is particularly important for the 1830s and 1840s copper bonanza. Centred on Caradon Hill, it was one of the most dramatic episodes in Cornish industrial history, and had crucial knock-on effects on local demography, agriculture and transport systems. The Moor's best preserved and largest complexes of mines, with shafts, adits, engine houses, horse whims, platforms and dressing floors, etc are found in this area.

By the mid to late 19th century many granite quarries had also been established, meeting the demand for carefully cut hard stone used in major public works, including docks, lighthouses and London bridges. Industrial hamlets developed near the more important quarries. Everywhere on the Moor are traces of the more casual removal and splitting of surface moorstones for such uses as gate-posts, lintels, and millstones.

China-clay extraction and processing (exploiting decomposed granite, or kaolin) developed here from the 1860s, though less intensively than around St Austell. The early Bodmin Moor clayworks are particularly interesting because they are often unusually well preserved.

The quality of archaeological preservation on Bodmin Moor is due partly to the use of granite in buildings and field banks, but also because of the relatively non-intensive use of the upland both in the recent past and today. The higher ground, even in times of better climate, has always been vulnerable to lower temperatures, heavier rainfall, stronger winds and has

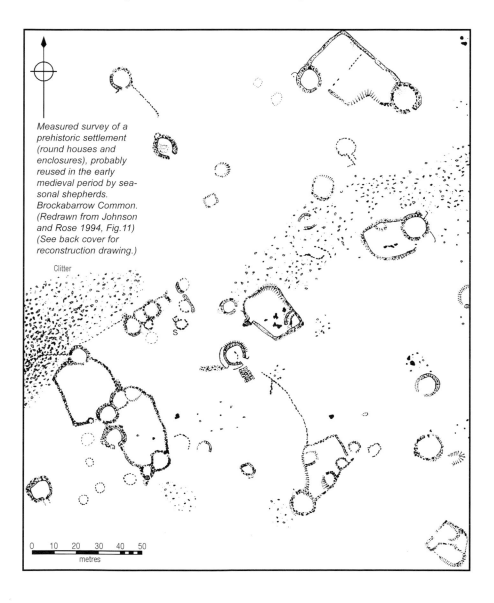

Measured survey of a prehistoric settlement (round houses and enclosures), probably reused in the early medieval period by seasonal shepherds. Brockabarrow Common. (Redrawn from Johnson and Rose 1994, Fig.11) (See back cover for reconstruction drawing.)

Clitter

0 10 20 30 40 50

metres

proved more suited to rough grazing than to prolonged cultivation. Consequently the imprint made by past peoples on the Moor remains much as it was left, whether it be a stone circle or prehistoric house, a herdsman's shelter, or a roughout for an 18th century millstone. As in the past, the future survival of this heritage depends on the moorland farmers and their continuing tradition of non-intensive farming practices.

Unlike Dartmoor, Bodmin Moor received little attention from early antiquarians and archaeologists. Their main interest, around the turn of the century, was in recording the stone circles. Apart from continuing recording work by the Ordnance Survey, and a campaign of excavation at Garrow by Dorothy Dudley in the 1950s, little was done prior to a series of 'rescue' excavations in the 1960s and 1970s. Bodmin Moor is neither large nor very elevated compared to most British uplands. Just twelve miles across, and rising to 1375 feet (420 metres) at Brown Willy, it is mostly above 800 feet (240 metres). Being small it is vulnerable to change, which at the turn of the 21st century tends to be uncompromising and irreversible. Agricultural intensification, conifer plantations, the construction of reservoirs and expansion of extractive industries, the contributions of our own complex modern world, have, together with the enclosures of the 19th century, reduced the moorland to just 95 square kilometres (37 square miles). What remains is often very fragmentary, especially in the southern part of the Moor. Sometimes the opportunity has been taken to excavate for archaeological remains in advance of such changes, for example at Stannon clayworks and on the site of the Colliford Reservoir. In the 1980s a major survey project by the Cornwall Archaeological Unit, English

Surveying the remains of a medieval longhouse on Louden Hill.

A longhouse (right) and barn under excavation at Bunning's Park in advance of flooding by the Colliford Lake reservoir

Heritage, and the Royal Commission on the Historical Monuments of England mapped the archaeological remains in detail over the whole Moor, using both aerial photography and field survey.

The object of this booklet is to use the results of this comprehensive survey to tell something of the story of Bodmin Moor and to describe and give a context to the many different features to be encountered. The study of Bodmin Moor is in its infancy and it is in the nature of archaeology that this story will develop over the years as ideas change and more information becomes available, particularly from further excavation. Research by Plymouth University, for example, has shed light on the changing environment, and University College London has investigated the prehistoric landscape at Leskernick.

The booklet is not intended as a guidebook; visitors to the Moor are recommended to use the Ordnance Survey 1:25,000 Explorer map (No 9) which covers most of the area, as it includes much of the new survey detail. **The visitor must remember that the moorlands, though appearing wild, are a component of managed farmland. Even common land is privately owned, and where there is no designated access permission must be sought from the farmers, landowners, and Commoners Associations.**

Hunter-gatherers of the Mesolithic Period 8500-4000 BC

As temperatures rose after the last ice age and an arctic, tundra-like vegetation was gradually replaced with woodland and scrub, small groups of hunter-gatherers moved northwards into Britain across a land bridge that was not submerged by the rising melt-waters until about 6000 BC. They would have found the exposed upland of Bodmin Moor a bare heathland, surrounded by scattered birch woodland on the lower ground. Gradual but dramatic change over the next thousand years saw a development both in the tree cover and in the resources which it would have provided. Most of Cornwall became shrouded in dense forest, mainly of oak and hazel. On Bodmin Moor however the exposed conditions held back the afforestation to little more than half the area. Whilst a birch, oak and hazel woodland grew in the more sheltered valleys, hazel scrub thrived on exposed hillsides. Much of the highest ground, however, remained open heather moor and upland grassland. In many valley bottoms, peat bogs developed throughout the period. Pollen blown from the surrounding vegetation and preserved within these bogs provides a record of this sequence of environmental change.

Much of the equipment of the hunter-gatherers would have been of perishable materials and has not survived: hides and skins for clothes and bags; wood for tools, bows and arrow shafts; bone for personal ornaments and tools; plant fibres for cords and baskets. If it were not for the fact that they also used flint, which is virtually indestructible, their presence on Bodmin Moor would be all but untraceable. Scatters of their flint flakes and artefacts are found in ploughed fields and exposed in eroded footpaths or at the edges of reservoirs. Characteristic of the period are small worked flints called 'microliths' which would have been used as the points and barbs on arrows and other projectiles.

Dozmary Pool. Hundreds of flint tools, including tiny microliths, have been found on the shores of this tarn-like lake, a focal point of Mesolithic hunting and gathering activity on the Moor.

Detailed studies on Butterstor (and on the Lizard peninsula in west Cornwall) suggest that large and small scatters can be expected. These represent both seasonal base camps, overnight shelters used in hunting forays and even more short-lived activity areas where animals were butchered or tools fashioned. Thousands of such sites must exist on Bodmin Moor, though few as yet have been located.

Judging by studies made of modern hunter-gatherers, these people would have had sophisticated traditions and beliefs. Although life may sometimes have been hard, they would have been completely in tune with their environment in a way that is difficult to imagine today. They knew how and when to exploit the riches it offered, the roots, berries, nuts, plants and fungi, the red deer and beaver, the wild cattle and pig, fish, seals and shellfish. To do this they may have moved camp in a seasonal cycle, based on the coast in the autumn for example to hunt the seals and their young pups; and in the summer months hunting red deer on the more open uplands.

First Farmers of the Neolithic Period 4000-2500 BC

By about 4500 BC farming had been introduced to Britain, either through an influx of new peoples or, as is increasingly being suggested, adapted by the native British. Any changes on Bodmin Moor may well have been very gradual, with the balance only slowly shifting from hunting to the grazing of herds and flocks. The woodland cover was steadily reduced but as yet it is impossible to say whether part of the upland was cultivated at this date, and whether permanently occupied settlements were established. As before, settlement sites of some sort are indicated by scatters of flints, including characteristic leaf-shaped arrowheads. Traces of buildings, hearths and pits may well survive beneath these scatters.

At a surprisingly early date, during the fourth millennium BC, hilltop enclosures appear. Examples excavated further west, at Carn Brea and Helman Tor, may have been major tribal centres used for ceremonies, and for exchanging material and ideas. Three or four sites on Bodmin Moor may be comparable, though as yet they are undated. They might instead be contemporary with the surrounding round-house settlements and Bronze Age ritual monuments. These are at Roughtor, Stowes Pound, De Lank (the latter poorly preserved) and perhaps Berry Down, St Neot. At Roughtor, lines of up to four very tumbled stone ramparts link the granite outcrops to enclose an area of 6.5 hectares (16 acres). Inside can be seen a few levelled platforms to take buildings, presumably of timber. Stowes Pound is even more remarkable. A massive stone rampart forms a small enclosure on the hilltop itself. Adjoining it to the north is a much larger enclosure (5 hectares; 12 acres), with a less substantial rampart, containing over seventy building platforms like those at Roughtor. Elaborate entrances lead in from both east and west. Just 2 km south-west of Stowes Pound a much smaller

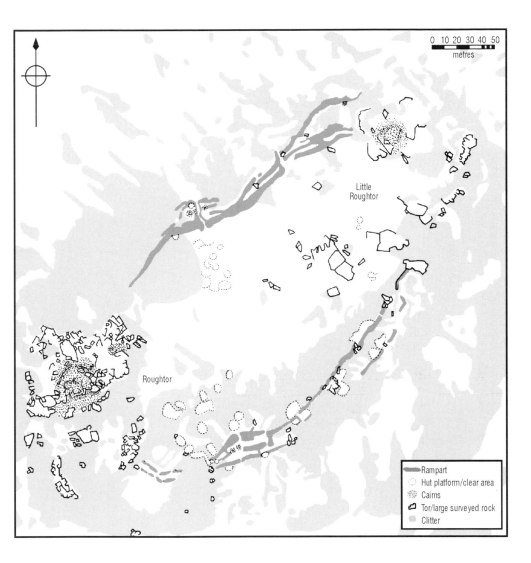

Hilltop enclosure on Roughtor formed by rocky ramparts running through dense clitter (areas of granite boulders) to link significant tors, which were later enhanced by large Bronze Age cairns. Probable hut platforms and other areas cleared of stone can be identified. (Redrawn from Johnson and Rose 1994, Fig.31)

enclosure with traces of a stone bank surrounds Tregarrick Tor and again contains cleared platforms. Another poorly preserved example may exist on Notter Tor, a similar distance to the north-east.

The standing stone is part of the north-eastern facade of the trapezoidal Neolithic long cairn on Catshole Downs. It appears to have been carefully aligned on Catshole Tor to its north-east.

Such monuments show the growth of a sophisticated and organised society. Also of the fourth millennium BC are the chambered tombs and long cairns. Best known is Trethevy Quoit, an awesome portal dolmen built on a southern finger of the granite upland. The monument is set in a low mound which probably never did more than cover its base. The three or four long cairns now known on Bodmin Moor (including Louden and Catshole) are rather less striking. Typically they are slight elongated mounds 17 to 30 metres long, sometimes with traces of internal structuring, though the original nature of this is usually obscure. In one case, at Bearah Common, there is a substantial but collapsed chamber. Similar sites elsewhere in Britain have been found to act as repositories for multiple burials, usually of only fragmentary skeletons. It is thought that, as well as being used for ritual and ceremony, the monuments would have represented a community's ancestral claims to the land on which they were built. On Bodmin Moor such sites may reflect territorial division of the upland from an early date. It is not known whether their builders lived in settlements nearby or off the upland, with the long cairns marking areas of seasonal upland grazing.

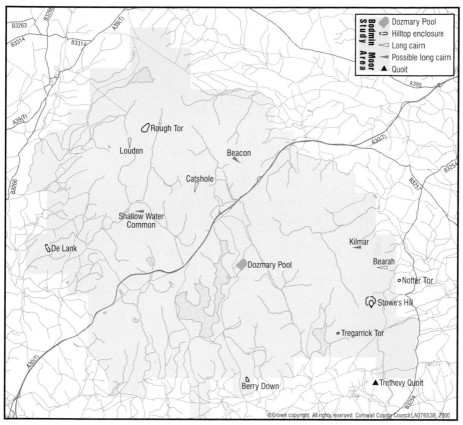

Early Neolithic sites on Bodmin Moor (Study Area Shaded). NB Some or all of the hilltop closures may be Bronze Age. © CAU/CCC

A number of apparently deliberately propped slabs, some with long axes pointing at significant tors (like Roughtor or Stowe's Hill), have recently been recognised on Bodmin Moor's tors. Their associations suggest a Neolithic date and their design reinforces the importance of natural features in the Neolithic world of ideas.

Stowe's Hill from the north-west. The small pear-shaped summit enclosure, defined by a massive stony bank partly lost to the Cheesewring granite quarry, has the character of a citadel but may have been a ritual enclosure. Its interior, containing many beautifully weather-sculptured tors, was neither visible nor accessible from the much larger lower enclosure on the rounded plateau in the foreground which contains scores of roughly circular house platforms.
© *CAU/CCC*

Ritual and Ceremonial Monuments of the Late Neolithic to Early Bronze Age 2500-1500 BC

Few periods, if any, can be represented by such a profusion and variety of ceremonial monuments as is the Early Bronze Age. On Bodmin Moor these are the stone circles and stone rows, menhirs and stone settings, and the cairns and barrows (mounds of stone and earth respectively). This phenomenon conjures up a picture of a society in which religion or ritual was a major and inseparable part of everyday life, fundamental to the way in which people perceived their world. Certainly their ritual sites - their equivalent of chapels, churches and shrines - were all around them in the landscape they grazed with their herds and flocks.

Of course religion is concerned with more than just matters of the spirit. It may also be the means of giving a community coherence and identity. One of the functions of the ritual monuments may have been to forge a sacred link between the community and its land. At a more mundane level, the distribution of the monuments throughout the whole of the upland suggests that its use had intensified enormously. Virtually every block of land (as defined for example by prominent hills and divided by rivers and streams) is marked

Showery Tor. A ring cairn was built around the natural cheesewring of weathered granite slabs.

by a group of cairns, as if all the available land was claimed and accounted for. The analysis of fossil pollens from the ancient land surfaces sealed beneath excavated cairns shows that by this date the upland was predominantly open grassland, with woodland confined to the steep valley sides.

The quality of survival on Bodmin Moor allows an exceptional opportunity to look at the way monuments relate to one another, to prehistoric settlements, and to the landscape. The ritual monuments are very often found in much the same area as the settlements and field systems, but in some places they are located a little apart, giving the impression of 'ritual' or 'sacred' areas. This term seems particularly apt where there are groupings or 'complexes' of ritual monuments. These areas had a double and perhaps inter-related value. Here people came for their ceremonies and religious observances, whilst their livestock could be grazed on the extensive rough pastures in which the monuments were set. Perhaps the location of the ritual monuments reflects the economic importance of the livestock, and the land on which they depended.

At present it is difficult to know whether the nearby settlements are actually contemporary with the ritual monuments - in many cases they are probably not. The ritual monuments, individually or in complexes, may well mark areas of seasonal grazing associated with particular communities. Whether these people lived close at hand, on slightly lower ground nearby, or even off the upland entirely, is usually unclear.

The ritual monuments are a part of the landscape not just by virtue of their sheer numbers but in the way they are sited in it. This can be seen most dramatically at Showery Tor (north of Roughtor) where the granite, outcropping in an impressive tor, is surrounded by a massive cairn of piled stones. It is as if the living rock were being

A well defined cist, missing its nearer endstone and capstone, in a cairn on the southern slopes of Louden Hill.

venerated and the natural world encompassed into the works of people. Because the setting is often integral to the monument, this adds a dimension that cannot be conveyed by plans or descriptions but has to be appreciated in the field.

Although most of these ceremonial monuments are not closely dated, several cairns and barrows have now been excavated and dated by the radiocarbon method, giving a range almost entirely between about 2000 and 1600 BC. This may well reflect the main period of activity involving the ceremonial monuments, though one excavated barrow, on Davidstow Moor, was found to contain a type of late Neolithic pottery known as Grooved Ware (c2500 BC). It is quite possible that the stone circles and stone rows, as yet undated in Cornwall, have their origins in the third rather than the second millennium BC.

Some 400 cairns are recorded on Bodmin Moor, a quarter of Cornwall's total. What is more, they represent a variety in size and type not found elsewhere in the county, where only the larger cairns, those over 10 metres in diameter, tend to survive. On Bodmin Moor the majority are under 10 metres. Diameters can range from under 3 metres to 34 metres, and heights from just a few centimetres to 3 metres. The construction of the larger cairns may have involved many people for many days, but the smallest could have been built by a handful of people in a few hours. Such diverse monuments clearly played quite different roles, and this is also borne out by their siting. The larger examples tend to be more prominently sited on ridges and hilltops, and some can be seen for miles around as pimples on the skyline (eg Carburrow, Brown Gelly, Tolborough, Ridge); presumably this was intentional, sites like Showery Tor or Alex Tor suggesting that the hilltop cairns were to be regarded as artificial tors. One of the several roles of such cairns may well have been as

A complex cairn, with concentric external and internal walls, under excavation on Stannon Downs in 1999. © CAU/CCC

territorial markers for a community. The smaller cairns, on the other hand, are generally inconspicuously sited, often on hillslopes, and closer to the round-house settlements, sometimes within their field systems. Perhaps these served small family groups. Their varying relationships with landscape features, other monuments, and activity areas indicate that the ritual and the domestic were inextricably intertwined in the Bronze Age, as they are still today.

The cairns and barrows are normally found in groups, some dense, some more dispersed, which must have expanded over the years. Good examples of groups of larger cairns may be seen on Brown Gelly, Langstone Downs, Carburrow, Bray Down and Buttern Hill. Groups of smaller cairns can be seen on the north-west slopes of Roughtor, and on Louden Hill.

An imaginary grouping of Bodmin Moor cairns showing some of the variety in final forms. © Rosemary Robertson

Most cairns (over 300 of them), as seen today, appear to be simple mounds. The rest have a range of structural features or components visible. A common feature is a revetting kerb of upright stones ('kerbed cairn'). There are also about forty examples of 'platform cairns', in which the principal component is a low, flat mound or platform. This may be further elaborated by a mound placed on the platform, or a bank around the rim, or both. Tor cairns, such as Showery Tor, Tolborough Tor, and Roughtor, incorporate a natural outcrop in their structure (eleven sites). Some fifty sites, mostly smaller cairns, have remains of a cist, a slab-built stone burial box, typically 1.0-1.6 metres long.

On excavation the cairns invariably prove to be more complicated than is apparent from field survey alone. Most can be expected to contain a range of structural features, including kerbs, inner kerbs, stone ring-banks, inner cairns, and cists. The 'enclosure' element is frequently found to be an important aspect in the original layout, presumably defining an area within which ceremonies were performed, a similar concept to that of the stone circles. For example, a stake circle 21 metres in diameter underlay a platform barrow on Davidstow Moor; and a stone ring-bank underlying a small cairn at Stannon originally had an entrance gap.

Rites and ceremonies leave their traces beneath cairns and barrows as spreads of charcoal, pits (often containing charcoal), and sometimes human cremations. Artefacts are rare: occasionally an urn, and perhaps a few flints and worked stones. Human burial is a key feature in some cairns. The best known example is the Rillaton Barrow (the largest on Bodmin Moor), where an individual was buried with prestigious artefacts: a bronze dagger, an urn and the famous gold cup. It must be stressed, however, that the majority of excavated cairns contained no human cremation at all. It seems that the

Small Bronze Age cup of beaten and corrugated gold found alogside a bronze dagger, glass beads, and other fine artifacts within the cist inserted into the eastern side of the large and prominent Rillaton barrow.

A large but damaged Bronze Age pottery urn (cracked and missing a handle) reused as a container for two human cremations. It was found upside down in a pit beneath a small cairn on Stannon Down.

deposition of human remains was just one amongst many rites performed at these sites, and so to call them all 'burial mounds' would be inaccurate.

The other classes of ceremonial monument mostly have upright stones as a common characteristic. The stone circles are the best known of these, but remain enigmatic though evocative monuments. Some may have been deliberately sited to observe the movements of the sun and moon as their rising and setting marked the seasons in their circuit of the surrounding hills. For example, from the Craddock Moor circle on Midsummer's Day the sun rises over Stowe's Hill and sets over Brown Willy. Such 'special effects' should be seen as just one facet of these sites, whose prime function was to enclose an area for the public performance of ceremonials.

The sixteen known stone circles are broadly similar in character, but differences in size, shape (ie regular or irregular circles), and stone size hints at the existence of distinct local traditions across the Moor. In two cases there are multiple circles. Best known are the Hurlers, a line of three large circles, with possibly a smaller fourth circle uphill to the north. There is also a pair of small circles on King Arthur's Downs.

The central and northern rings at the Hurlers triple stone circles.

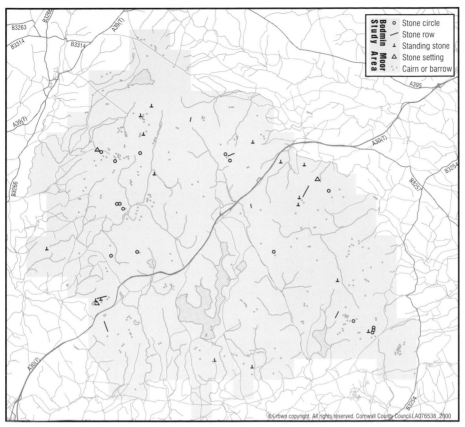

Distribution of Later Neolithic and early Bronze Age ceremonial and ritual monuments. Not all would have been contemporary with each other, or with the prehistoric settlements shown (for clarity) on a second map. © CAU/CCC

The Stripple Stones circle is unique on Bodmin Moor. Here the stone circle is set within a henge, an embanked ritual enclosure which has its ditch inside the enclosing bank. Though continuing in use in the second millennium, henges belong mostly to the third millennium BC.

Bodmin Moor's stone circles, and the henge, seem to have been carefully located in the landscape. For example nearly all were placed so that visually dominant tors were to their north, and for nine of the sixteen circles this was Roughtor, the beautiful high hill with the early prehistoric enclosure, a focus of many instances of clever Bronze Age landscape design. A good and typical example involves the Trippet and Stripple Stones. Both have Roughtor as the principal skyline feature and the henge's entrance is positioned to allow people within to see the Trippets, confirming linkage between the two sites. Anyone walking from the Trippets to the Stripple Stones soon lost sight of Roughtor as they crossed a stream and passed to the south of Hawk's Tor. Roughtor remained invisible until the moment the bank and ditch of the henge were crossed; by the time the centre stone was reached the great hill dominated the northern sky.

Part of the Trehudreth Downs stone row with its typically small and unimposing stones.

Stone rows have only recently been discovered on Bodmin Moor. Eight are now known compared to seventy or so on Dartmoor, though others will probably be found. The stones are often very small and easily obscured by patches of gorse or thick peat. All are single rows, ranging in length from 12 to 560 metres. The stones tend to be either small and closely spaced (eg Trehudreth Downs, and Craddock Moor), or larger and further apart (Colvannick, and East Moor). Their function is obscure though their linear character may hint at a use in processions. The careful landscape designs which influenced their location and orientation worked mainly as people moved along them. Some rows are in ceremonial complexes which include stone circles and other monuments, but most are well apart from the circles. If the circles and rows are ceremonial centres for groups using the area surrounding them, their distribution, at intervals of about 1.5 kilometres, suggests that the upland was divided into a series of fairly small 'territories'.

Menhirs, or standing stones, are not such a feature of Bodmin Moor as they are of West Penwith. There, excavation has shown that burials were sometimes placed at their base. In Wales menhirs have proved to be just the above-ground component in

The Advent Longstone, a Bronze Age menhir or standing stone nearly 3m high. Roughtor is prominent on the skyline.

complexes which include paved areas, stake-built structures, and burials. This should be expected in Cornwall as well. Some of the fifteen examples known are typical of what one expects of menhirs, large individual stones up to three metres high (eg The Longstone, Advent). Others, however, are much smaller - some under a metre high - or are closely associated with other monuments; for example there are paired menhirs, and menhirs within cairns, or set at their edge.

The term 'stone setting' has been used for a handful of monuments involving settings of upright stones, but they are all quite different. A staggered line of four small uprights is set 60 metres north-west of the Stannon stone circle. Next to a cairn on Trehudreth Downs is a setting of three uprights in an arc, as if to define a forecourt-like area where rites could be performed against a backdrop of distant hills under the great expanse of the upland sky. Another class of monument allows a special insight into prehistoric practices; these are the two

Stone setting on Trehudreth Downs, apparently part of a complex which included the nearby stone row and several cairns.

'embanked avenues' which may well have been used in processions. Each is formed by two banks of stone, 4 metres apart in one case, 8 metres in the other, and 60 metres and 87 metres long, respectively. One leads from the west directly towards the impressive tor cairn at Showery Tor. The other is a component in the major complex found in the Craddock Moor - Cheesewring area. The north-west end of this embanked avenue points towards one end of the Craddock Moor stone row. Its south-east end points directly towards the Craddock Moor circle 550 metres distant, and the projected line continues to intersect the Hurlers stone circles. In this way the avenue forms a link in a remarkable prehistoric alignment. Also in this area are numerous cairns, including the Rillaton Barrow, and the great defended settlement of

An embanked avenue climbing towards Showery Tor.

Stowe's Pound.

The Craddock Moor/Hurlers complex is the most impressive of those found on Bodmin Moor, and may have been of more than local importance. There are other complexes at Leskernick which includes two stone circles, a stone row, and cairns; and Trehudreth Downs which has a stone row, stone settings, menhirs and cairns and East Moor: with stone circle, stone row, cairns. Roughtor was, as noted above, the focus of many ritual and ceremonial monuments, from the three north-western stone circles to cairns and propped stones as far away as Carburrow Tor, 12 kilometres to its south.

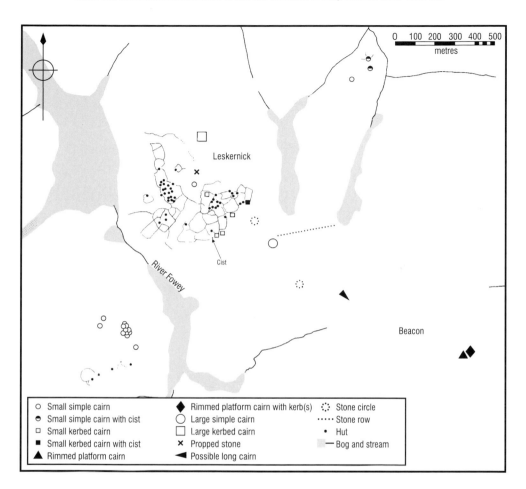

Leskernick area showing relationships between Bronze Age ritual sites and set-tlements and enclosures. Features may not be contemporary but note how there is some separation of larger monuments away from settlements but also much intermingling of ritual and apparently secular features. (Redrawn from Johnson and Rose 1994, Fig.28)

Prehistoric Settlement in the Second Millennium BC

How the prehistoric settlement on the western slopes of Brockabarrow Common may have looked when occupied (see plan in Introduction).© Rosemary Robertson.

A persistent theme, in prehistory and later, is the changing balance in the character of land use on Bodmin Moor, between seasonal grazing and permanent settlement. The seasonal grazing probably included the practice of transhumance. People would have moved onto the upland in May with their flocks and herds and lived there with them during the summer months before returning in October to rejoin the rest of the community in their settlements in the lowlands or nearer the edge of the Moor. These upland settlements would have been not just a vital part of the economy but also home to a large part of the community for half the year. Probably there was a continual shift of emphasis, with some areas only ever used for seasonal grazing and transhumance but others fluctuating between temporary and more permanent use. This helps to explain the great variety seen in the types of settlement.

There are some 1500 prehistoric round-houses on Bodmin Moor in approximately 200 settlements. Though virtually undated here (only three sites have been excavated), they are assumed, by analogy with Dartmoor, to belong predominantly to the second millennium BC. However, pottery of the Iron Age, belonging to the first few centuries BC, was found in excavations of reused Bronze Age round houses at Garrow, St Breward, and at Stannon, St Breward, where excavation in 1999 has shown that a house was built inside a Bronze Age ring cairn. Sometimes there is evidence for several phases of activity and this, together with the variety of the settlements, suggests a long time span. It is likely that many of the settlements are not contemporary with the ritual monuments that are often found near them so we must be wary of seeing Bodmin Moor as a coherent Bronze Age landscape.

The internal diameter of round-houses ranges from 2 to 12 metres or more, giving an enormous variation in floor area from $3m^2$ to $113m^2$. The typical round house has a diameter of 5 to 7 metres; this would give a floor area of $20m^2$ to $35m^2$, similar to the living area of a medieval longhouse (18-$40m^2$), and would presumably have been adequate for a family. On this analogy the smaller houses, particularly those under 4 metres in diameter, are unlikely to have housed a family, but may have been used for individuals, or for short periods only, or may have served as animal houses or stores. At the other end of the spectrum, round-houses with an internal diameter of 12 metres would have a floor area around three times that of the living accommodation of a medieval longhouse. These were very substantial buildings. The traditional term 'hut circle' hardly does justice to these structures: 'round-house' is increasingly used as an alternative, though this is also not entirely satisfactory as the smallest structures are indeed hut-like! The fact is that no single term can adequately represent the range of prehistoric buildings, any more than such a term could be used to encompass, at a later period, everything from a hen-house to a manor house.

The typical round-house is slightly levelled into the hillslope and sometimes built out a little from it, and is defined by a circular stone bank broken by

A Bronze Age round house on Stannon Downs being surveyed

an entrance gap. The wall or bank usually has traces of an inner face, formed by slabs set upright or on edge, or sometimes by coursing. Where there is an outer face it is generally less pronounced, simply marking the tail of the bank. The wall would have supported the rafters of a steeply pitched conical roof, probably thatched. Entrances may be simple breaks in the perimeter, or defined by upright stones acting as door jambs. Sometimes the wall is thicker and better built at the entrance, or may be protected from the elements by a little porch or shielding bank. The house walls can be substantially built or no more than very low stony banks. Sometimes where there is only a circular platform to be seen it is possible that the house was built entirely of wood, without stone walls at all. Excavation on Dartmoor has shown that timber houses are quite common. There may well be hundreds of them on Bodmin Moor as yet undiscovered.

Within the house may have been one or more hearths, probably set on a stone slab, although excavation of houses at Stannon found no indoor hearths. It did, however, show that all sorts of stake-built internal fittings can be expected, such as partitions and the supports for benches and beds around the perimeter.

Reconstruction of a round house at Trewortha Farm, based on information gathered from excavations on Bodmin Moor. (Reconstruction designed by Tony Blackman and Graham Lawrence.)

Settlement size ranges from single isolated houses to clusters of over ninety, though most have fewer than twenty. The main types of settlement are:

Unenclosed settlement (no fields or enclosures) (29 examples)

Settlement with small enclosures (16-35 examples)

Settlement within an enclosure or enclosures (5-8 examples)

Settlement with a field system (122 examples).

There are also two settlements of quite a different type which may be of this period - these are the remarkable hilltop settlements of Roughtor and Stowe's Pound, described previously, which could be either of Neolithic or Bronze Age date.

The fields associated with the round-houses are generally curvilinear in shape and accretive, that is to say the field system can be seen to have grown, with successive fields added one to another. The field boundaries are typically low curving banks of stones or boulders, sometimes with a build-up of soil at the bottom of the field giving evidence for cultivation. On

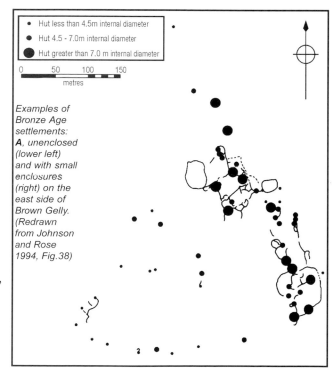

Examples of Bronze Age settlements: **A**, unenclosed (lower left) and with small enclosures (right) on the east side of Brown Gelly. (Redrawn from Johnson and Rose 1994, Fig.38)

- Hut less than 4.5m internal diameter
- Hut 4.5 - 7.0m internal diameter
- Hut greater than 7.0 m internal diameter

0   50   100   150
metres

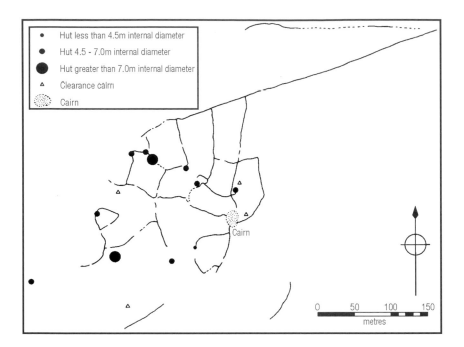

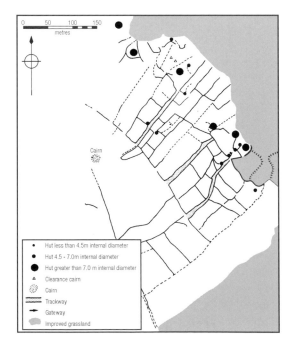

*Examples of Bronze Age settlements: **B** (above), with curvilinear field system on Lady Down; (Redrawn from Johnson and Rose 1994, Fig.41)*

__C__ (right), within rectilinear field system on Carne Downs. (Redrawn from Johnson and Rose 1994, Fig.42)

Bodmin Moor the number of houses tends to be large in proportion to the area enclosed by fields, compared for example, to West Penwith where large clusters of houses are unusual and instead they are scattered in ones and twos through extensive field systems. The differences may be due to a greater emphasis on pastoralism on Bodmin Moor, including transhumance, though prehistoric tin streaming may also be a factor.

Settlements which have no fields at all, or just small enclosures, are quite likely to have been transhumance settlements, or if permanently occupied must have been

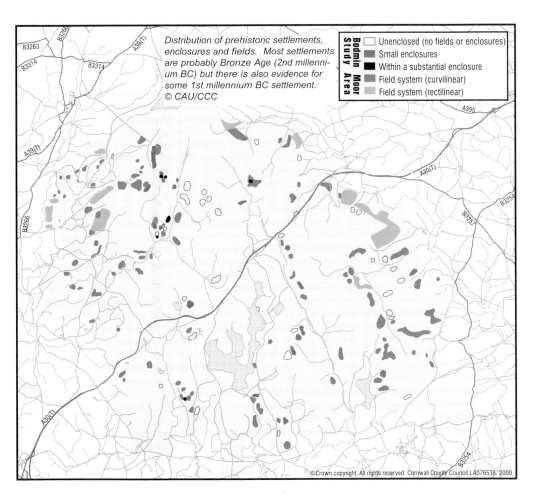

Distribution of prehistoric settlements, enclosures and fields. Most settlements are probably Bronze Age (2nd millennium BC) but there is also evidence for some 1st millennium BC settlement.
© CAU/CCC

Bodmin Moor Study Area
- Unenclosed (no fields or enclosures)
- Small enclosures
- Within a substantial enclosure
- Field system (curvilinear)
- Field system (rectilinear)

specialised pastoral settlements interdependent with communities who put more emphasis on growing crops. These settlements are quite variable in character: at some the small roughly-built houses are very likely to have been in only temporary use; but others have large well-built houses (eg Brockabarrow), which could have been permanently occupied.

Part of the Bronze Age rectilinear field system above Tolcarne on East Moor. Two round houses are clearly visible, as is medieval cultivation ridging.
© CAU/CCC

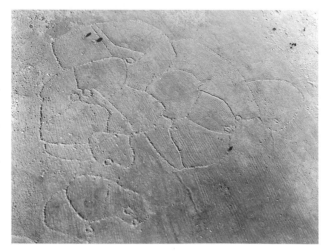

Curvilinear field system on Craddock Moor. Individual farmsteads with one or two round houses and two or three fields accreted on to each other can be identified. Lanes took livestock to the unenclosed ground beyond. Medieval cultivation ridges are visible in most fields and in the open moor downhill.
© CAU/CCC

Particularly around the edges of the Moor there are more extensive rectilinear field systems (those with fairly straight boundaries, enclosing generally rectangular fields) which have a more planned and cohesive layout. These and other more fragmentary field systems on the fringes of the upland may be more typical of the permanently occupied settlements of the surrounding lowlands.

Other field systems take the form of widely spaced boundary banks dividing up tracts of pasture into large blocks. By analogy with the Dartmoor 'reaves', which comprise boundary banks and rectilinear field systems set out over hundreds of hectares, these might date from around 1700-1600 BC. It should be noted that though sharing the concept of dividing and organising the landscape they are not directly comparable in layout, being much smaller in scale and paying more heed to the local topography. The use of the boundary banks suggests the need for closer definition and control of the pastures, and closer definition of property and commons, perhaps to cope with increasing pressure on the available resources.

In some cases boundary banks can be seen to overlie earlier field systems, thus demonstrating changing land use during prehistory. For example, a clear sequence has been identified in the

A typical prehistoric stony bank on the western side of Roughtor.

Roughtor/Louden/Stannon area. Here there are at least three phases: a series of curvilinear accretive field systems (see above), probably associated with scattered round-houses (initial colonisation and cultivation?) is cut by a boundary bank system (c1600 BC?) which may be associated with settlements with small enclosures and limited field systems (transhumance and relatively intensive pastoralism?). In a subsequent phase (first millennium BC?) a large settlement of small houses (transhumance camp?) on Louden Hill cuts one of the boundary banks. (The dates suggested are working hypotheses only.)

Later Prehistory

Bury Castle, a later prehistoric hillfort on the south-western side of Bodmin Moor. A second defensive line of rampart and ditch, at the most vulnerable uphill, northern side, has been largely ploughed down but was visible in the evening shadows when this aerial photograph was taken. © CAU/CCC

It is currently assumed that most settlements were abandoned by c1000 BC, due to deteriorating climate and impoverishment of the soils, and that the use of the upland was less intensive in the first millennium BC. It is likely that some round-house settlements are transhumance camps of this date, and there are many instances of round houses with later small structures built within them, suggesting reuse as temporary shelters. The only readily identifiable settlements of later prehistory are the strongly defended hillforts (c400 BC - AD 50; Bury Castle, Cardinham, and Berry Castle, St Neot) and the rounds - enclosed farming settlements defended by a single bank and ditch (c400 BC - AD 600). Excellent well-preserved examples can be seen at Allabury and Bray Down. The sites are found fringing the Moor or occasionally along the valleys, and avoid the main granite upland, which served as a great tract of seasonal grazing.

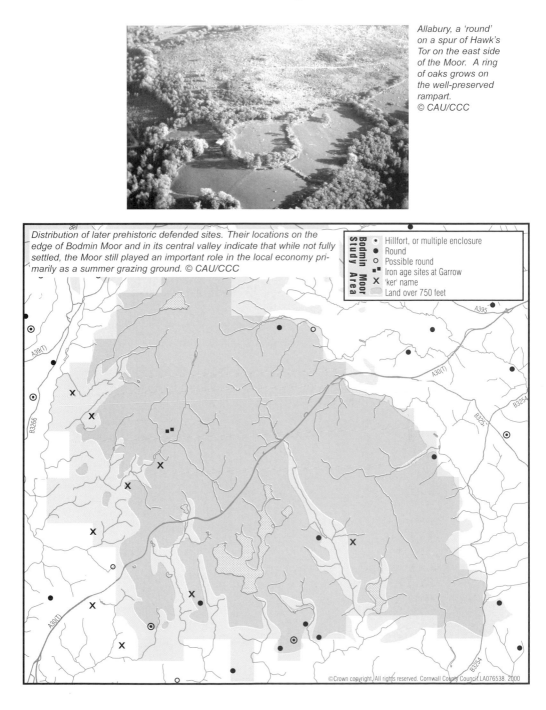

Allabury, a 'round' on a spur of Hawk's Tor on the east side of the Moor. A ring of oaks grows on the well-preserved rampart.
© CAU/CCC

Distribution of later prehistoric defended sites. Their locations on the edge of Bodmin Moor and in its central valley indicate that while not fully settled, the Moor still played an important role in the local economy primarily as a summer grazing ground. © CAU/CCC

Bodmin Moor Study Area

- • Hillfort, or multiple enclosure
- ● Round
- ○ Possible round
- ▪■ Iron age sites at Garrow
- X 'ker' name
- ▨ Land over 750 feet

Medieval Bodmin Moor
AD 400-1540

The Cornish name for Bodmin Moor, recorded only once, in the 12th century, was Goen Bren, meaning something like 'open common downs of a hill'.

Place-name and documentary evidence suggests that medieval colonisation of the Moor had begun by the 11th century, spurred on by a process of population growth that continued until the savage blows of the Black Death in the 14th century. It is clear that pre-Norman settlement avoided the granite upland almost entirely. This is also true of the Early Christian inscribed memorial stones (5th to 7th centuries AD), the parish churches (generally on sites of pre-Norman origin), and places recorded in Domesday Book (1086). More importantly, places with Cornish settlement names of early type likewise form a ring around the upland. These are places with the elements tre and bos, meaning 'farm, estate, or hamlet' and 'dwelling' respectively (eg Trehudreth and Trebartha, Bowithick and Bofindle).

By contrast settlements on the granite upland mostly have either English names (eg Fernacre, Smallacoombe, Langdon) or Cornish topographical names, ie names derived from hills and such like (eg Garrow and Brown Willy). Settlements with the early Cornish elements tre and bos would date anywhere between the 7th and 11th centuries and may even be older. Likewise, the paths and sunken lanes that link the settlements, and elements in the field systems that surround them, are likely to be equally ancient. Something of the nature of this landscape can be seen in Domesday Book - the large areas of pasture recorded, and woodland mostly in the south and south east, where fragments of the ancient woodlands survive today, preserving a pattern that probably goes back into prehistory.

Looking down on Cardinham church-town and the wooded valleys and mature lowland farmland beyond from Bury Castle, at the edge of the parish's upland downs.

The medieval and early medieval manors and parishes were arranged in such a way as to include both well-settled lowland and upland moor. Before its colonisation Bodmin Moor would have offered some 200 square kilometres of rough pasture, ideal for seasonal grazing; and would have been used as such by the surrounding settlements. Slightly-built rectangular buildings found on the Moor both individually and in groups may have been used as shelters and temporary homes. This continues a tradition of transhumance stretching far back into prehistory. A good example of a group of such buildings can be seen on Brockabarrow Common, and a single elongated building stands 150 metres east of the Stannon stone circle, though with its rounded ends it may be Romano-British rather than medieval. Occasionally all animals were rounded up and checked and those found to be grazing the moors illegally would be held in pounds such as that which survives as King Arthur's Hall in St Breward parish.

Over a hundred medieval settlements were established on Bodmin Moor, mostly spreading up valleys such as the Fowey and the De Lank, but also into woodland areas east and south of the Moor. This is borne out by numerous settlements with English place-names referring to woods, clearings and groves. Most of these farming settlements have continued in use to the present day but over thirty are now deserted. The process of desertion began in the 14th century, not necessarily because moorland communities were obliterated by the plague but because with the drastic reduction in population the more productive holdings that became available in lowland

Reconstruction of the upper part of the medieval longhouse hamlet at Brown Willy, showing how the co-operative set-tlement was made up of several indi-vidual farmsteads. © Rosemary Robertson.

Cornwall were quickly taken up at the expense of those in the uplands. Some places were probably abandoned more or less at once but most commonly they continued in use on a smaller scale. Hamlets of four or five farmsteads would be reduced to just one or two, and in some cases in the course of the succeeding centuries these too came to be deserted.

The medieval layout can still be seen at many of the deserted settlements (eg Louden; Lamlavery, on Davidstow Moor, and Carwether, in St Breward). The outline of the rectangular buildings is marked by ruined walls or grassy banks and one can normally see little enclosures that would have served as gardens, mowhays (rick-yards), and penning areas. Some of the settlements are single farmsteads but most are hamlets of from two to six farmsteads, clustered together around or through a small open area or 'townplace', a shared farmyard. Hamlets, which were the characteristic settlement type in medieval Cornwall, both in the lowlands as well as on Bodmin Moor, were a combination of the private with the communal. The individual households form distinct units, but their close grouping would have enabled them to work together in many aspects of the seasonal round. The Bodmin Moor hamlets were probably all much of a similar status, relatively humble farming settlements belonging to a manor; the manor houses tended to lie off the Moor, or at its fringes. A rare example of an abandoned fortified manor house, or very minor castle, known as Upton Castle, survives in woodland on the north-east moorland fringe; a defensive wall on a small knoll encloses two buildings, one of them probably the hall.

The uniformity and predictability of the layout of the hamlets is in quite striking contrast to the diversity of the prehistoric settlements, which had a greater time span and more varied functions. Each farmstead in the medieval hamlet consists of a main farmhouse, usually a longhouse, and one or two smaller out-buildings - barns and animal houses. The buildings are almost invariably all set with the long axis running down slope, presumably to help drainage.

The main characteristic of the longhouse is that it housed under one thatched roof both the living accommodation for the household, and the shippon for the wintering of livestock, almost certainly cattle. There was access between the two through a cross-passage that ran across the middle of the house. The shippons, as we know from excavated examples, had mangers of wood or granite slabs built against the walls, and a drain ran down the centre. (The shippon is invariably at the lower end of the house!) The living room or hall, open to the rafters and with a central hearth and fittings for benches and beds against the walls, acted as kitchen, dining room and bedroom,

Four well-preserved medieval longhouse hamlets:(from the top) Carwether from the north-east; Lamlavery on Davidstow Moor from the north-east; Brown Willy from the west; and Trewortha Marsh from the west. © CAU/CCC.

though often an inner room beyond gave more space for storage and beds. At best there would be just narrow slits for windows.

Documents give us a much fuller picture of the medieval landscape, which allows us a view of the social contacts of the moorland folk that is not possible for prehistory. For someone in a hamlet, after the links with their own family and household, would come daily contact with immediate neighbours in their own hamlet, and more occasional contact with their neighbours in the surrounding hamlets. A visit to church on Sunday would be a chance to trade gossip with the rest of the parish, and likewise with attendance at the regular manor courts. An outing to one of the surrounding market towns - Bodmin, Liskeard, Launceston and Camelford - meant rubbing shoulders with people from a much wider slice of Cornwall, as well as the business of buying and selling.

The pattern and form of the hamlets and fields probably reflect the contemporary practice in lowland Cornwall, up to the 14th century, transplanted, with adaptations, to an upland granite landscape. The farms and hamlets invariably had fields associated with them. Unlike the prehistoric settlements, they included large areas under crop, at least until the 14th century when the fall in population both on the Moor and in Cornwall generally, resulted in more specialised farming practices, with pastoral farming predominating in the uplands. Before this, the main crops would have been oats, rye and pillas, a type of oats.

Cultivation ridges ('ridge and furrow') can be seen widely over Bodmin Moor and extended even to some of the highest and most inhospitable ground, for example on the upper slopes of Brown Willy. This gives some idea of the pressures on land in the medieval period for although temperatures are thought to have been slightly higher up to the 14th century, the dampness of the climate, the wildness of the weather, the rockiness of the ground, and the thin acid soils gave the medieval farmer a great deal to contend with. The success of the crops may often have been precarious. At some

Stone clearance onto an earthfast boulder in medieval outfields on Roughtor.

settlements small corn-drying barns can be recognised, with traces of the kilns and ovens used to dry the wet or unripe grain prior to threshing and grinding.

The cultivation ridges served to provide a seed bed in the thin soils and helped drainage. The narrow ridges (usually under 3 metres wide), often sinuous and irregular, were probably made by a mixture of spade-digging, especially where the ground is rockiest, and by ploughing with a small team of oxen. A very common sight are clearance heaps of small stones cleared from the fields and piled onto earth-fast boulders.

Some twenty or so deserted medieval settlements have near-complete survival of their contemporary fields. Commonly the farmers would enclose their land with one or more long, curving boundaries (usually a bank with a ditch outside), within which part of the area would have been cultivated and the rest used as pasture. For example, Brown Willy, a hamlet of five or six long-houses, had 270 hectares (675 acres) of enclosed land of which some 53 hectares (132 acres) were cultivated. Much of the arable on Bodmin Moor (but not all) was subdivided as strip fields, defined by low stony banks, and this formed the local variation of open field cultivation. Each farmstead in the hamlet would have its share of strips scattered through the fields. At Brown Willy the field system began with two fields divided into a total of seventeen strips. Each strip was 108 feet wide (33 metres) ie six Cornish rods of 18 feet. Subsequently the system expanded by creating further blocks of strips. (The Brown Willy fields can be seen clearly from the summit of Roughtor, but are not publicly accessible.)

Undisturbed medieval strip fields in the foreground and others beyond 'fossilised' by reuse of alternate boundaries in the working farm of Fernacre.
© CAU/CCC.

Only parts of the field system would have been cultivated at any one time. Most of the medieval fields to be seen on Bodmin Moor are more fragmentary remains surviving within or beyond field patterns which have otherwise continued in use to the present day. Many of these abandoned fields are probably the result of temporary or 'outfield' cultivation.

A form of convertible or ley husbandry was probably used in the main part of the field system. This involved 2 or 3 years of arable followed by 4-9 years of grass, the seeds of which were sown with the last arable crop. The dense turf which developed during the grass phase was skimmed off with hand tools, and then dried and burnt. Its ashes were mixed with dung, sea-sand and other dressings before being scattered onto the bare ground prior to digging or ploughing.

Most of the field systems of medieval origin on Bodmin Moor, and elsewhere in Cornwall, have remained in use, and although the actual form of the boundaries has changed over the centuries and boundaries have been removed or added, the 'modern' hedges or walls generally fossilise elements of the medieval layout, including strip fields. In this way much of the fabric of the medieval countryside still survives. (As a rule of thumb, slightly curving, sinuous or irregular boundaries will mostly be medieval, and dead straight lines will be 19th and 20th century enclosures.)

The lane to the Moor from Treworra medieval hamlet in Davidstow.

Although a great deal was cultivated, huge tracts were still rough pastures. These were either enclosed pastures associated with specific settlements or the open commons. The latter would have been of great importance to both moorland farms and also many settlements surrounding the Moor. They were used as pasture and for collecting fuel, either as turves (peat) or furze (gorse). Ferns (bracken) would be cut for bedding. People living in the lowland parts of Altarnun parish had rights on West Moor and East Moor. Some of the small rectangular buildings seen surviving on the moors as very low foundations may well be shelters or temporary dwellings for medieval herdsfolk.

Numerous lanes and trackways led from the surrounding farms up onto the moors, and when new farms were carved out of the moor in the medieval period care was taken to prevent the

new enclosures from blocking the routeways. The uplands were criss-crossed with tracks: major thoroughfares, as well as trackways leading to moorland farms, and descending to lowland farms. Sometimes the traveller was guided by a granite wayside cross, set up as a marker post to show the way off the moor or point the direction across it (eg Long Tom, St Cleer; the Middlemoor Cross; Fourhole Cross); other crosses marked the path to church. South of Bodmin Moor the old road from Launceston and Liskeard to Bodmin is carried by a series of ancient medieval bridges where it crossed the rivers and streams running off the Moor (eg Panters Bridge and Treverbyn Bridge, St Neot).

The fine churches of the moorland parishes are almost all set in the lower fringes and form a ring around the upland. Most are on sites which were in use for Christian worship long before the Norman Conquest. The two Early Christian inscribed memorial stones at Lewannick date from the 5th or 6th centuries, and its raised oval churchyard or lann is probably equally ancient. Cardinham churchyard contains an early inscribed stone and an impressive ornamented cross of the 10th century. St Neot is recorded in Domesday Book having a small religious community, and in the churchyard can be seen what is probably the earliest cross in Cornwall, an elaborate ornamented shaft of the 9th century. Other chapels, sometimes with holy wells associated, are likely to be of early medieval origin, though the superstructure of the wells is medieval or later (eg the well known sites at St Clether, St Cleer, St Neot, Davidstow, and St Breward, and Teason holy well, Cardinham).

Top: Middle Moor Cross which guided medieval travellers crossing Hamatethy Commons in St Breward © Andrew Langdon.
Bottom: The 10th century ornamented cross in Cardinham churchyard.

St Clether holy well from beside the chapel.

Exceptions to the general trend are the little church at Temple, thought to represent a colonisation by the Knights Templar in the 12th century, and the chapel of St Luke's, again in the heart of the upland, which at one stage had parochial status and would have served the hamlets that had spread up the Fowey (its precise site is now lost).

Temple church as rebuilt in the late 19th century on the original cruciform plan. The medieval original may have been erected by the Knights Templar; it is close to the ancient Launceston to Bodmin road over the Moor.

In 1371 licence was granted to Sir Hugh Peverell (Lord of Hamatethy) to have service in the chapel of St Michael the Archangel 'atte Roghtorr' (Roughtor). The foundations of the little chapel can still be seen on the summit, placed there perhaps as a beacon of Christianity amidst a throng of pagan relics.

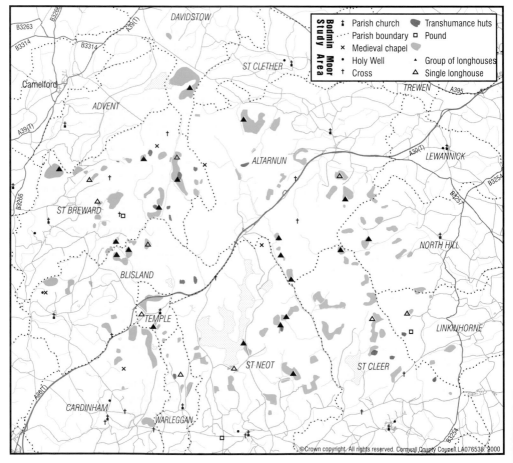

Distribution of selected medieval sites on Bodmin Moor. © CAU/CCC.

Medieval
Industry

Known in the later medieval period as Fawymore or Foweymore, from the river which rises near Brown Willy and whose valley bisects the uplands, Bodmin Moor (as Foweymore Stannary) was, along with Dartmoor and Blackmore (around Hensbarrow), one of the South-West's most important tin producing areas by the 12th and 13th centuries. It was, however, declining by the 14th and 15th centuries as easily worked deposits were becoming exhausted by the streamworkers and miners began to work lodes directly. One consequence of this intensive industry was that silts and sands from the streamworks were redeposited downstream to the extent that Lostwithiel, a major port of the 12th and 13th centuries, could no longer accommodate sea-going vessels by around 1400. This medieval pre-eminence of Bodmin Moor was not a short-lived boom but rather the tail-end of a long period of successful tinning. Pollen analyses of valley bogs tied in with radio-carbon dates suggest that some streamworks now drowned by the Colliford reservoir were worked in the Iron Age or Romano-British periods. The discovery in early modern alluvial streamworks of later prehistoric artefacts means that we should not be surprised to find Bronze Age workings surviving on Bodmin Moor.

Recent survey has located many well-preserved examples of each of the two main types of streamworks, alluvial and eluvial. The former exploited deposits of cassiterite (tin dioxide) detached from lodes, subjected to weathering and transported by various processes to valley bottoms where alluvial action had sorted it, the cassiterite being considerably heavier than granite. To reach the cassiterite the streamers manually removed the overburden, usually peat first and then stones and silt deposited by later water action. This might be up to 10 metres deep, and the dumps of unwanted 'stent' produced alongside or downstream from the working areas or 'tyes' can be correspondingly large. A variety of patterns of dumps and tyes has been recorded.

Simple circular pits with arrays of dumps around them (as on East Moor) are possibly prospections while other patterns, like the series of roughly parallel slug-like heaps (as at Cannaglaze) created by throwing stent up with shovels or the ranks of low gently ramped heaps (as at Carneglos), formed by using wheelbarrows, are likely to be the products of systematically working deposits. Alluvial streamworks, found in valleys where streams still flow, are now usually waterlogged and have growths of peat over them. The streams had to be temporarily diverted from the working areas and diversion channels can still be found, again usually waterlogged (good examples at Shallow Water Common). Drainage channels, however, are no longer visible; these received the water carefully fed by streamers through their tyes to remove, in suspension, the fine waste from the layers of cassiterite, usually on wooden boards or

Medieval eluvial streamworks on West Moor showing leats running into the main cutting from the lower left and the dams of reservoirs alongside it in the upper right. Patterns of spoil heaps on the cutting's floor reveal the organisation of working areas or tyes. © CAU/CCC.

buddles, and will now usually be several metres below the modern stream level. Although some of the finest alluvial streamworks were drowned by the Colliford reservoir a number of excellent medieval examples survive on Bodmin Moor, for example in the several valleys on West Moor in Altarnun parish. Several alluvial streamworks have been disturbed by post-medieval reworkings; those at Brown Willy, Blackadon and Bowithick, among others, continuing into the 20th century.

Eluvial streamworks have generally suffered less post-medieval disturbance. These worked 'shode' (detached and weathered cassiterite not thoroughly sorted by alluvial action) and are usually found in dry valleys or on hill slopes. As they tend not to be waterlogged and have limited peat formation over them, features are fairly clearly defined.

Working methods were similar to those in alluvial works with water run through excavated shode placed on boards in the tyes taking off the lighter waste materials. Collecting and storing this water was often a major problem and these works are usually associated with long leats and numerous simple reservoirs (good examples on Penkestle Moor and West Moor). Richard Carew writing in the early 17th century marvelled at 'how aptly they [the Cornish tinners] cast the ground, for conveying the water, by compassings and turnings to shun such hills and vallies as let [hinder] them, by their too much height or lowness'. The main cutting of an eluvial streamworks usually runs downslope and can be up to 18m deep (as at Buttern Hill) but is usually between 1 and 4m deep. Within it are dumps of stent, their patterns echoing those of the tyes. Variety in these patterns was deliberate, the streamers carefully creating ideal angles of slope to ensure that the flow of water through the tye was sufficient to carry off waste but did not also wash away shode. Drainage channels survive in most of these streamworks. Good examples of eluvial streamworks survive in all parts of the Moor (Penkestle, Redhill, Long Tom).

Where water could not be easily collected to operate streamworks, for instance on hill tops and on high plateaux, areas of shode would be dug over with small 'dry' pits to create 'shambles' of shodeworks (as on Goonzion Downs). Such shambles are often found adjacent to eluvial streamworks, at their upper ends, higher than the point where water could easily be brought (eg Cardinham Moor). The excavated shode-bearing ground would be taken downhill to water for cleaning or dressing.

Small and simple tinners' buildings, drystone or turf built, shelters and stores, are often found either within or alongside both kinds of streamworks. We are still not sure whether the workers were part-time local farmers or full-time tinners; those huts beside the more remote streamworks could have sheltered either. The effect on local agriculture

A ruined tinners' shelter with small gable-wall fireplace next to the Roughtor Ford streamworks.

of a vibrant industry bringing both wealth and, perhaps, a workforce needing food into the area must have been great and it has been suggested that the increased commercialism of the later medieval period helped stimulate the rise of the confident individual farmer and the decline of the communal farming hamlet.

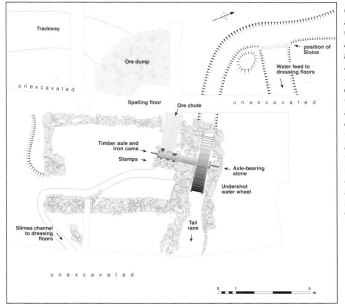

Colliford stamping mill showing excavated walls, leats and wheelpit and with a reconstruction of the wheel, stamps and ore chute. Such sites crushed ores obtained from openworks, lode-back pits and shodeworks as part of the dressing process which separated the heavy tin from the lighter waste materials. Stamping mills were also used on shaft mines right through to the 20th century.
© Rosemary Robertson.

Tin was smelted in the later medieval period in blowing houses scattered around the moorland edges where fuel and strong-running streams were plentiful. Waterwheels worked bellows serving stone-built furnaces fed with wood or turf charcoal. Few are known to survive in Cornwall; that at Coombe being the best example on Bodmin Moor, a rectangular building with a wheelpit and a displaced mortar stone (for reworking slag). More often only floatstones (shallow granite troughs in which molten tin accumulated during the smelt), mouldstones (in which the ingots were cast), or scatters of slag (black glassy product of reduced ore) are found. Finally the ingots were taken to the 'coinage' towns (Lostwithiel and Liskeard) where tax was paid prior to their transport to many different markets, both national and international.

Agriculture and Settlement from the 16th century

There are two quite distinct strands to the post-medieval settlement history on Bodmin Moor: purely agricultural settlements, usually with medieval origins, and industrial settlements; the small farms, cottages and hamlets occupied by families of mine, quarry and china-clay workers.

Medieval hamlets in the early post-medieval period had mostly shrunk to just one or two farms and their previously open field systems had been enclosed with Cornish hedges to allow individual farmers to work their land as they thought best. The communal system had broken down. New farms, such as those on the exposed downs of St Breward, places like Casehill, Whiteheads, Irish and Palmers were also solitary farms. Evidence from the 1695 Lanhydrock Atlas and the c1840 Tithe Maps confirm that agriculture was still mixed, with convertible or ley husbandry being practised. Each field was cropped for 2 or 3 years before being put down to ley grass for 6 to 10 years. The old strip field systems were adapted to this and the new ones laid out for it with 10 to 15 roughly square fields.

Most post-medieval and modern Bodmin Moor farmhouses were relatively modest; the tiny 17th-century house at Leaze in St Breward, with one main room up and down, was not a cottage but a farmhouse as was the equally small ruined house at Bedrawel, nearby in Blisland, with its chamfered lintels and jambs. Farm buildings, barns, cowhouses, piggeries etc, were also small and simply built, reflecting the poverty of post-medieval farming in this marginal land.

Dryworks, an early modern farmhouse with farm buildings attached. The slate cladding is unusual on Bodmin Moor.

More substantial houses and buildings are found on the wealthier farms at the moorland fringes, places like Lank, Hamatethy and Carne.

Many moorland farms have been abandoned in the 20th century as the holdings, often with less than 30 acres of enclosed and improved land, plus some rough grazing and rights to commons, were too small to be viable, especially after the late 19th-century shift to specialisation in beef or dairy farming. Farms were thrown together but amalgamation's goal was the land, and the unwanted buildings were often left to decay into poignant monuments to recent struggles. These abandoned farmsteads, nettles and brambles growing in the rubble of fallen roofs and collapsed walls, buzzards nesting on cold chimney tops, have become important archaeological sites, repositories of information about fairly recent but still quite simple agricultural methods and ways of life. Little imagination is needed to repeople these sites.

The dwelling is often located slightly away from the main farmyard, often an apparently irregular grouping of barn, cowhouse, stable, cartshed and piggery although analysis reveals how animals, fodder, dung and milk were efficiently moved around the site. A vegetable garden, a mowhay (yard for ricks of corn, hay, bracken and turf) and perhaps a small orchard form the farmstead enclosures, often medieval in origin in the older farms, between which lanes weave their way to the fields and the world beyond. You may find primitive, but modern, stone built farmstead structures; multipurpose small sheds built as beehive huts, common in north-west Bodmin Moor, and gooseholes and kennels built into the bases of hedges or farm buildings.

Mid 19th century challbarn at Carkeet. Cattle and horses were housed on the ground floor and grain was stored and threshed (using waterwheel-driven machinery) on the first floor.

One of two beehive huts at Leaze farmstead, St Breward.

Many farming settlements only survived because of the effects of industry on the moorland economy. Farmers or members of their households supplemented the farm's income and produce with wages, or returns from the sale of ore or stone. Others benefited from the wealth brought into the area by industry and commerce and the associated demand for foodstuffs.

Many more settlements were established to house the families of industrial workers, especially in the later 18th, the 19th, and the early 20th centuries. Some were plain cottages

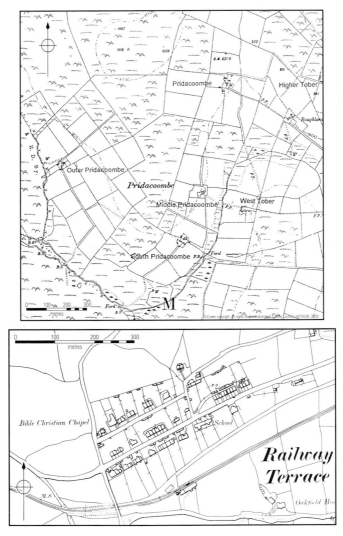

Intake fields and farmsteads, mainly established in 1837, in the Pridacoombe area of Altarnun.

Industrial workers' housing at Railway Terrace, now known as Darite, as mapped in 1906, showing a mix of individual cottages and terraces or rows.

grouped into hamlets, either expanded ancient ones like Henwood, Darite and Row or wholly new ones like Cheesewring Railway (now Minions) and Watergate. There were also isolated cottages and many rural terraces or 'rows' such as that now demolished at Cheesewring quarry.

Of particular interest are the new smallholdings of the early 19th century. Cut out of unenclosed moors and leased on favourable terms to agricultural and industrial labourers, many of these small farms have survived into the 20th century and make a significant impact on the moorland landscape. The first tenants were often obliged to build within one year dwelling, stable and barn and to hedge in fields which had been laid out by the landlord's steward. These distinctively rectilinear fields can be seen in the Moor's bleakest corners, along Pridacoombe's sides, around Lord's Waste, Pinnock's Hill and Colquite, at Edenvale and Camperdown and, most remote of all, on Smith's Moor and at Rushyford Water. Acreages were limited, rarely more than 20 acres, dwellings small and low, often under the same roof as the barn and stable, and the easily poached peaty soil often muddy. Although the rough ground ensured a pastoral bias the

View south across 18th and 19th century intake farms at Higher Penhale, Trevillian's Gate and Oldpark to the open commons of High Moor and Davidstow Moor. Brown Willy (left) and Roughtor dominate the view. © CAU/CCC.

agriculture practised by these small farms was still mixed as the surviving threshing barns, horse engine platforms (for powering crop-processing machines) and staddle stones (for corn rick stands) make clear.

A turf stead on Davidstow Moor.

Full use was made of the landscape, as it also was at the more ancient farms. The rough ground and commons provided more than summer grazing. Ferns (or bracken) were cut for bedding, furze (or gorse) for the quick baking heat, and most importantly of all turf (or peat), was cut or dug for homely warmth and the ready cup of tea. Turf dried alongside the cuttings was stacked in ricks through the summer before being brought down to the homestead in the autumn. Hundreds of the turf steads on which the ricks were built survive, typically rectangles c7m by c3m with shallow ditches and low banks around. Extensive groups exist on Bodmin Moor downlands, for example on Pridacoombe Downs.

On the open moors, remote from fields and tinworks, are a number of ruined post-medieval dwellings, cabins rather than cottages, small, single-storeyed, and often with gable-end chimneys. They were apparently used by herds people or other moorland workers, perhaps seasonally. Elsewhere there are several tiny temporary shelters, barely large enough to lie down in, some perhaps stores, usually drystone built and often tucked inside prehistoric hut circles or against large rocks. They are difficult to date and interpret but are assumed to be post-medieval and again the products of herds and those others who moved across the moors, peat-cutters, stone-splitters, rustlers and poachers.

Post-medieval Industry

Tin and copper

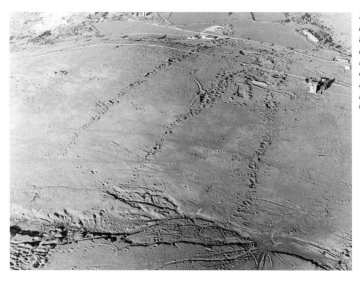

Strings of lode-back pits crossing the downs between the Hurlers stone circles (lower right) and Rillaton barrow (upper left). © CAU/CCC.

Towards the end of the medieval period tinners began to turn their attention from alluvial and shode deposits to the lodes themselves. Bodmin Moor contains many important early lode working sites. An openwork (narrow opencast quarry cut along a lode) at Colliford appears to have been dug by the 15th century and others in the southern half of the Moor may be as early. So too may be some of the lode-back works, lines of closely spaced primitive shafts strung out along lodes, now mostly slumped to become large pits up to 15m diameter and 5m deep. These shafts may have been interconnected by levels below the surface and a few have alongside them the circular platforms of horse engines, used for winding up spoil and ore and perhaps for lifting up water. Excellent lode-back works survive on Goonzion Downs,

Hardhead Downs, and on the moor north of the Hurlers. They represent the beginning of the move underground which in the early modern period resulted in the more familiar deep tin and copper mines, based on shafts and adits.

Shaft and adit mines were probably rare in Cornwall and on Bodmin Moor before the 16th and 17th centuries. Streamworks and the surface workings of lodes (openworks and lode-back pits) required much less investment and, exploiting clearly visible deposits and veins, were less risky. These deposits and veins were, however, becoming exhausted. While shaft mines, often sunk into the unknown and suffering the twin problems of primitive and inefficient rock-breaking methods (fire-setting and picking) and difficult drainage, were risky adventures, the steadily increasing demand for tin forced miners underground and their technological problems were gradually overcome in the 16th, 17th and 18th centuries. Rock-breaking was speeded up by the introduction of gunpowder (probably by the 16th century) and drainage was eased by the driving of adits, horizontal tunnels run from lowlying ground, usually a nearby valley bottom, and then, from the early 18th century, the use of steam engines to pump water up from greater depths to adit level. These engines and other forms of mechanisation enabled Cornish mines to develop rapidly in the 18th and 19th centuries and to participate fully in the so-called Industrial Revolution. Several well-preserved early mines organised around adits and simple shafts served by horse engines and waterwheels survive on Bodmin Moor including Wheal Dorothy, Trewint Moor, and Bray Down.

The century from 1785 saw Cornwall's non-agricultural economy dominated by metal mining. As well as tin, copper, a mineral not widely sought in earlier times, was extensively worked for. The Minions and Caradon area in particular was the scene of a copper bonanza in the 1830s and 40s with the spectacular success of the

Holmans and Rules Shafts, with dumps and ruined engine houses, on the great South Caradon copper mine, viewed from the south. The higher of the two parallel lines is a mineral railway. © CAU/CCC.

Clymos and Kittows at South Caradon Mine bringing in the
enthusiasm and capital to allow West and East Caradon,
Phoenix United, Marke Valley and Craddock Moor Mines to
flourish. Some mines, particular Phoenix United, were able to

*The Minions area in
1905 showing the
industrial village,
then called
Cheesewring
Railway, set among
the 19th century
mines (most already
disused by 1905),
quarries and rail-
ways, which had led
to its development.*

ride out the collapse in copper prices after c1855 by returning
to tin production. Although the boom which made south-east
Bodmin Moor one of Cornwall's most important mining
centres ended abruptly with the arrival of cheap foreign tin in
the later 19th century, a few mines struggled into the 20th
century. Strategic minerals such as wolfram were also mined
here and elsewhere on the Moor during the two World Wars.

Away from the Minions area, Bodmin Moor mines tended to
be relatively small, sporadically working poor shallow lodes
mainly towards the edge of the granite. Wheal Bray, Roughtor
and Lemarne Mines, the great openworks at Treveddoe or
Wheal Whisper, Wheal Hammett and Hobbs Hill are among
the best preserved. Their small scale and their distance from
good transport networks, and thus from easily obtained
supplies of coal, timber and machinery, led to the continued
use into the later 19th and even 20th centuries of sources of
power for pumping, winding and processing which would have
been common elsewhere in Cornwall in earlier centuries.
While steam engines became the principal power source in the
late 18th and 19th centuries in most of Cornwall and in the

Minions area (where some 120 of the 135 steam engines known on Bodmin Moor are recorded), water and horse power predominated over most of the rest of the Moor. Bodmin Moor mine sites are generally well-preserved and large numbers of waterwheel pits and horse engine platforms survive (good wheelpits at Treveddoe; horse engine platform at Wheal Dorothy). On the latter, harnessed horses turned vertical axles which either rotated overhead winding barrels or worked, via gearing and cranks, primitive pumps. If the power source was distant from where it was required (often the case with waterwheels), power could be transferred along flat rods supported by rocking bobs (good example at West Rosedown).

Mines were focused on shafts, used for pumping, access, winding and ventilation, although few performed all four functions. Ventilation shafts were simple draught openings cut upwards from underground levels but pumping and winding shafts normally had built collars and usually had power sources (steam engine, horse engine, waterwheel, or the angle-bob of flat-rods bringing in power) adjacent to them.

Draining deep mines required pumps to bring the water up to at least adit level. Early pumps, worked by waterwheels, horse engines or even manually, were crude and inefficient but by the later 18th century steam engines, larger waterwheels and even wind engines (at Vincent Mine in Altarnun) were operating pumping rods capable of keeping mines several hundred fathoms deep dry enough to work.

The last great mining engine house built in Cornwall, on Prince of Wales Shaft in Phoenix United tin mine. It was started in 1909 but closed just five years later.

The manual removal of ore, spoil and materials also rapidly became uneconomic as shafts deepened and where stuff could not be taken out through adits or levels it was hauled by machines. At first, in the 16th, 17th and 18th centuries, some mines may have had simple windlasses but it is likely that horse engines and waterwheels were used from the earliest times. In the 18th and 19th centuries rotative steam engines were also employed. These also often powered man-engines lowering and raising the miners themselves. Spoil would normally not be brought to the surface if it could be dumped underground, in worked out areas. Substantial surface dumps, usually finger-form with the lines of tramways or barrow-ways

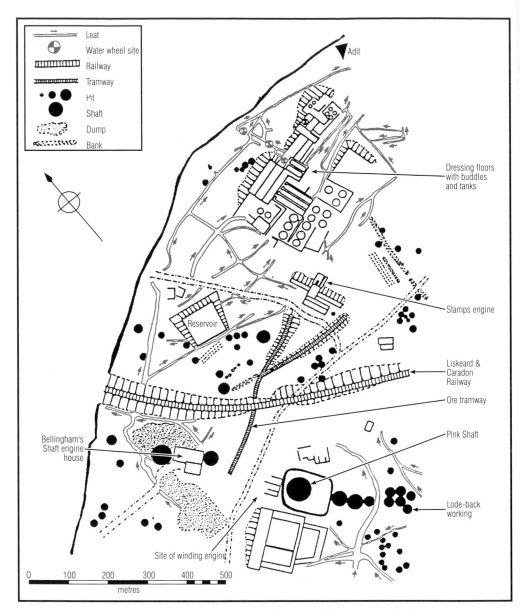

Leat
Water wheel site
Railway
Tramway
Pit
Shaft
Dump
Bank

Adit

Dressing floors
with buddles
and tanks

Stamps engine

Liskeard &
Caradon
Railway

Ore tramway

Reservoir

Bellingham's
Shaft engine
house

Pink Shaft

Lode-back
working

Site of winding engine

0   100   200   300   400   500
metres

The main shafts (with ruined engine houses) and late 19th-century tin dressing floors at Wheal Jenkin.

running along their backs, are usually either the product of a mine's earliest workings or an indication that the principal access was by an adit or a low-lying shaft.

The gaping shafts, dripping adits, and remains of the power sources for pumping and winding, the powerful and dramatic houses which contained steam engines, the wheelpits, and horse engine platforms, are all vivid reminders that a mine depended on work underground. It was, however, at surface that much of the mine's structural complexity existed, most notably the ore dressing plant. Here the excavated material was transformed by a number of stages into the relatively pure ores demanded by the smelting houses.

Most tin mines on Bodmin Moor had their own stamping mills and dressing floors and some survive in very good condition (eg Wh. Jenkin, Halvana). Bal maidens and boys using various hammers broke down ore-bearing stones on spalling floors uphill of sheds in which stamps (heavy iron-strapped timbers) were lifted and dropped by cams on a barrel axle turned by a

Four round buddles and, beyond them, a well preserved calciner building on the tin dressing floor at the western edge of Hardhead Downs.

waterwheel or a rotative steam engine. The spalled ore fed under these stamps was turned into a fine dust which with added water became a slime. This was a solution from which the heavy tin fell out quickly, leaving the waste to flow on, the same principle employed by the streamworkers. Agitating the slime in manually operated trapezoidal buddles (one survives at Treveddoe) and then from c1850 in mechanical round ones, and on shaking tables (as at Phoenix United) facilitated the separation. Material would normally be re-processed one, two or three times to maximise ore collection before the concentrated tin was roasted in the burning house or calciner to burn off unwanted arsenic, pyrites and other impurities (well-preserved reverberatory calciners can be found at Tresellyn and at Hardhead Downs). After a final re-buddling to remove solid by-products of this burning the tin ore was

dried and bagged ready for removal to the smelter as 'black tin' (ie c.60% pure tin).

Dressing, or processing, copper differed considerably from tin as the principal ore, chalcopyrite, was easily lost in water separation and was usually hand picked from the waste, both underground and on the surface. Lumps of 'drage' (ore mixed with gangue, or other unwanted minerals) were broken down by ragging with 10 lb hammers and then by cobbing or spalling, broken down finer by women

Early 20th century wolfram works at Bowithick Marsh. The massive V-shaped dam (upper left) formed a lake on which a dredger floated to work the alluvial deposits. A well-preserved dressing floor is visible downstream (centre). © CAU/CCC.

and boys using bucking hammers. In the late 18th century waterwheel-driven crushers were developed. Of a number of possible 19th-century crushing houses surviving on Bodmin

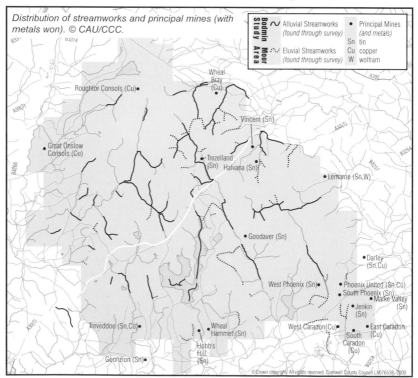

Distribution of streamworks and principal mines (with metals won). © CAU/CCC.

Moor that at Wheal Bray is probably the best. The crushed material was not as fine as tin slime and after agitation, 'jigging' in water, light waste and iron pyrite was skimmed off. Jigging was at first done manually but later hand-operated and water-powered machinery was developed.

The dressing floor, usually just a little way downhill from the main winding shaft or haulage adit, was, with the pumping shafts nearby, the nucleus of the mine. Other buildings clustered around it: the smithies and carpenters' shops providing and repairing tools, drills, sheds and props; the 'dry' in which the sweating and wet miners dried themselves and their clothes on returning to surface; and the count-house from which the clerks paid the miners and bal maidens and in which they dealt with the mine's accounts and where adventurers entertained potential investors. Tramways and trackways provided internal transport networks. Placed at a safe remove from this nucleus was the mine's gunpowder store, the small, solid, square magazine or powder house.

Quarrying

The granite of Bodmin Moor has been used in buildings and other structures since Neolithic times. In the later medieval and early post-medieval periods moorstones (the natural boulders scattered over the landscape) were split and dressed to make simple lintels, jambs and quoinstones, and also more difficult objects - crosses, millstones, arches, cider-millstones etc. Stone splitting methods developed over the centuries. Before c1800 a row of chiselled slots would take iron wedges, to be hit with sledgehammers until the rock split. After c1800 iron plugs were hammered into lines of hand-drilled holes, each fitted with a pair of iron feathers, until the granite broke away along the line (plug-and-feather splitting). Wedge-grooved and drill-marked blocks of granite are found in small irregular pits in all parts of the Moor as are unfinished or flawed millstones, crosses, troughs, staddle stones.

A cider apple-mill base-stone abandoned half-finished on Louden Hill.

Stone splitting and dressing was sometimes done by specialist masons rather than local farmers and in the early 19th century small quarries were opened, like that on Treswallock Downs, cut into the bedrock itself and yielding scores or hundreds of worked pieces rather than just the one or two obtained from loose surface moorstones.

The group of well preserved early 20th century granite dimension stone quarries on Carbilly Tor. Finger dumps of waster rocks are arranged downhill of the flooded pits.© CAU/CCC.

These quarries, producing stone for local markets, differed from those dramatic 19th and 20th-century excavations the dimension stone quarries, not just in scale but also in their object. Dimension stone was the carefully cut and dressed flawless granite used in major civil engineering works (lighthouses, piers, bridges, docks etc), in military installations, and in large public buildings. For example De Lank quarry supplied the granite for a series of famous lighthouses: Eddystone, Beachy Head, and the Bishop's Rock. The quarries, most of which are found towards the edges of the Moor, can be very large, over 100m across, and had either simple cuttings running into hillsides (as at Pendrift) or pits dug deep into their floors, searching for the best rock (as at Goldiggings). Such pits are usually flooded now. Above them rise vertical faces marked with the long charge-holes into which the gunpowder was tamped, and rows of plug-and-feather holes.

On quarry floors may be found traces of the cranes and derricks used to move the blocks around: stone crane-bases, the rings and chains used to secure them, even the cranes themselves (as at Corner Quoit quarry and Bearah Tor). The tramways laid out within the quarries to move around blocks and waste also ran out along the backs of the enormous finger dumps of waste rock, up to 100m long, 12m high which spread out onto the moors below the quarries (excellent examples at Carbilly). Smaller dumps of waste rock lie among the crane bases and dressing floors. In the latter are the footings of flimsy masons' sheds and the plinths which supported sawing, dressing and polishing machinery (again good examples at Carbilly). Smithies, where drills and other tools were made and sharpened, also often survive, and some way from the nucleus of the quarry can be found the powder house or magazine.

The finished stones had to be removed from the often remote quarries. Metalled tracks and tramways, sometimes inclined (as at De Lank, St Breward), were laid out connecting them to the docks and railways which transported the stone to local and distant markets.

Another form of large quarry found on Bodmin Moor is the late 19th and 20th-century roadstone quarry. Sources of ballast for road and railway, and perhaps also stone for local buildings and hedges, these exploited densely fractured granite and seams of elvan. They tend to be long and narrow, following the seams or lines of weakness, and have no dumps of waste rock. Everything but the overburden (the soil stripped off the bedrock) was taken and used. They also rarely have any associated buildings, although at De Lank where several roadstone quarries were worked alongside the famous dimension stone quarries, there is an abandoned stone-crushing mill.

Carbilly's north-western quarry.

Rab, gravelly decomposed granite (excellent material for surfacing tracks) was also quarried. The many flat-bottomed rab pits, usually found next to the tracks where the product was used are likely to be modern, few being known to date before the mid 19th century.

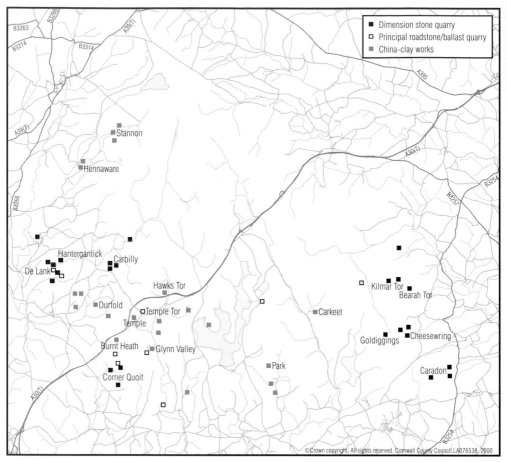

Distribution of china-clay works and principal granite quarries. © CAU/CCC.

China Clay

Another important later 19th and 20th-century industry on Bodmin Moor was the working of china clay, an essential ingredient of hard-paste porcelain and more recently used in paper-making, cosmetics and pharmaceuticals. Clayworks are confined to the western half of the Moor and although one is still operational (Stannon) the industry has been less successful here than in the St Austell china-clay area, or around Lee Moor on Dartmoor. It was also relatively late starting on Bodmin Moor with little evidence of pre-1860s working. Bodmin Moor china clay (kaolin; aluminium silicate formed on the decomposition of the feldspar in granite) is generally more micaceous and less easy to work than that of the St Austell district, and the Moor's remoteness from railways and the sea has always presented considerable transportation problems. Most of the 25 or so late 19th-century clayworks had been shut down before the First World War although a few were re-opened after it (Glynn Valley, Temple, Hawkstor and Northwood, as well as Stannon and Parson's Park). While Bodmin Moor's china-clay history was not sparkling,

Burnt Heath late 19th century china-clay works. Low finger dumps of waste were formed downhill of the now flooded pit. Circular and subrectangular settling tanks were positioned uphill to the right of the rectangular pan kiln. © CAU/CCC.

widespread failure has left many early complexes in good condition, whereas in the more important St Austell clay district, the later and current reworkings have either damaged or destroyed most 18th and 19th century pits, dumps and processing areas. Material remains of many aspects of this important industry (still one of the South-West 's principal employers) are therefore best seen here on Bodmin Moor.

China-clay extraction has always used water. In the earliest Bodmin Moor pits the 'stream and strake' method was employed. After the overburden and a discoloured layer of clay-bearing stone had been removed from a kaolin deposit (located by prospecting pits or trenches), a stream of water was directed over the exposed clay ground to take off the kaolinised material in suspension, leaving behind the unaltered rocks or stent in a gully or 'strake'. Workers, 'dubbers', standing in the stream, broke up this material with shovels and picks to ease out the kaolin which in the earliest hillside works flowed out of the lower end of the pit. As the pits deepened the liquid clay had to be removed from their bottoms by other means, by adits driven from the pit bases or by pumping through shafts. The pumps were either water-powered (eg the enormous Gawns wheel, 50 feet in diameter, which pumped, by flatrods, Temple clay works 1¼ miles away) or worked by steam engines (as at Northwood). Until pressure hoses were introduced in the 1920s all pits were worked by stream and strake and would have been served by complex leat systems bringing in the water.

Glynn Valley early 20th century china-clay works on the east side of Great Care Hill. Waste was trammed up conical sky dumps. Extensive dressing floors including settling tanks, mica drags and pan kilns were laid out downstream of the pit. © CAU/CCC.

Much of the separation of the kaolin from the other components of granite, quartz and mica, took place within the pits themselves, coarse gravel and sand being deposited within them as the clay flowed on. Pits were regularly cleared out, gravel, sand and stent being taken out by hand in the earliest, then by skip roads or inclined tramways powered by horse-engines, waterwheels or steam engines. Early dumps were flat-

Circular settling tanks in front of the pankiln's stack at the early 20th century dressing floor of Henneware china-clay works. © CAU/CCC.

topped fingers along which barrows and then, later, tramways trundled the waste (fine examples at Burnt Heath, and Colquite). These low dumps often covered ground which could itself be quarried, and the characteristic conical sky tips were developed to less wastefully dump spoil. These had powered skip roads, continually extended as the mountain grew (Glynn

Valley clayworks). Modern dumps, again ramped and flat-topped to allow dumper trucks access, dwarf both finger dumps and sky tips.

The liquid clay was further purified at surface. In early works it flowed through three stepped tanks in which sand, a mix of fine sand and mica, and then mica alone were deposited. These tanks were later refined into sand drags, deep, narrow channels, and mica drags, shallower channels (good examples at Glynn Valley works). The waste sand and thickened mica went on to the claywork's dumps, and liquid mica was impounded in mica lagoons to reduce pollution of streams and rivers.

Settling tanks removed most water before the clay was dried, at first very slowly in the open air in clay pans (air dries) and then, after c1850, in pan kilns whose tiled floors were heated by furnaces connected by hypercaust brick flues to chimney stacks (good example at Henneware). The dry clay, ready for sale, was transported by waggon, a major cost on Bodmin Moor with its agricultural lanes, and around 1900 a number of pipelines were laid to carry liquid clay to pan kilns built alongside railways, at Moorswater, Newbridge, Tresarrett and Wenford.

The active china-clay works at Stannon. © CAU/CCC.

Brickmaking was often associated with china-clay working, using poor or discoloured clay and providing bricks for domestic as well as industrial use; the latter included bricks used in the processing plant of clay works themselves (chimneys, furnace arches, pankiln floors etc). A well-preserved small brickworks survives, partially re-used as a farmyard, at Carkeet.

Communications, Chapels, Carved Stones

Industry brought many changes to Bodmin Moor. Communications were improved: a railway network serving mines and quarries was established in the south-east - The Liskeard and Caradon Railway, built in 1846 to Moorswater to link with the Liskeard and Looe Union Canal. Much of its trackbed survives, with setts and chairs, as do those of tramways serving various quarries and clayworks. Although later abandoned, many of these, together with metalled trackways, have been incorporated into the formal and informal systems of moorland roads and tracks. The main road pattern, however, is still the essentially medieval agricultural one with farm paths and tracks leading to local lanes and roads which then feed into thoroughfares and eventually highways. Most notable is the present A30 which splits the moor into two as it hurries people between Launceston and Bodmin along a route marked with medieval crosses and bridging, until very recently, the Fowey at a medieval crossing-place, Palmersbridge. Most of the tiny moorland streams were crossed by fords and causeways until the 19th century when many simple clapper-bridges were built using lengths of split granite. There are relatively few surviving pre-19th-century clapper bridges on the Moor. These have undressed granite

Simple early modern clapper-built footbridge linking Brown Willy with Butterstor.

slabs laid across crudely built piers; one links Brown Willy with Butterstor.

Increased religious nonconformity accompanying increased population on the Moor in the late 18th and 19th centuries produced numerous Methodist chapels (examples at St Lukes, Temple, Harrowbridge, Highertown) and then, with

the series of Education Acts from 1870,
elementary schools. These included the second
school at Bolventor, the hamlet originally called
Boldventure built up around Jamaica Inn in the
1840s by the improving squire Rodd of Trebartha
who provided it with a National School and
small parish church.

Bible Christian chapel in the clay-worker's hamlet of Highertown.

At Dozmary Pool is a ruined iceworks of the
freezing 1880s and 1890s. Ice harvested from the pool was
stored in a stone-lined platform cut into the hillslope on its
north bank by being covered with turves. In the summer a
turf-fuelled steam-powered machine compressed the ice for
use by south Cornish fishermen to keep their catch fresh on
the trains to London.

One of Daniel Gumb's several inscriptions made on granite rocks in the Cheesewring area.

A number of carved stones can be found on Bodmin Moor.
Daniel Gumb's 18th century geometric figures in the
Cheesewring area and the memorial near Roughtor Bridge to
the murdered girl Charlotte Dymond are famous, but less well-
known is the Jubilee Rock at Pendrift, Blisland which has
coats of arms of important landowning families carved
alongside those of George III and Victoria. To save the
picturesque tors, over a hundred fleurs de lys were carved in
1864 to indicate to stonecutters those parts of the Duchy
manor of Rillaton where they could not work. There are
numerous mainly 19th-century boundstones on the open moor
some with initials of owners more or less neatly inscribed.

The Military
on the Moor

Surviving Second World War stores and the concrete footings of others, including two aircraft sheds (for repairs and servicing) connected to the taxiing circuit of Davidstow airfield. Beyond the crossing runways are some of the node-like aircraft dispersals where bombers were parked between missions.
© CAU/CCC.

The modern armed services have had relatively little impact on Bodmin Moor compared with Dartmoor. There are lookout huts on several hilltops, most spectacularly at Carburrow Tor, and there were several searchlight stations on and around the Moor. Davidstow Moor's Second World War airfield is well preserved as is a 19th-century Volunteer rifle range at Lowermoor. Another small arms range on Fore Downs near Millpool is still used, with flags and striped poles on nearby hills marking the danger zone. American artillery positions, used for firing towards Brown Willy while training for D-Day, survive on Penkestle Moor and near Minions and some of their shell-holes can still be picked out. Infantry foxholes dot other areas of the Moor. Scraps of riveted aluminium can be found on the eastern slopes of Brown Willy, the remains of a bomber from Davidstow airfield which crashed here. The Liskeard-Caradon railway bridge at Minions was removed by the military to allow the passage of large trucks.

Conclusion

This booklet describes and interprets the physical remains of long periods of continuity and several major episodes of change on Bodmin Moor. It shows how people have usually been influenced by the structures and spaces left by previous occupants. Monuments have been seen as the products of understandable cultures with which people have had a basic sympathy, whether they were Methodist chapels, medieval houses, or prehistoric fields and ceremonial monuments. The visible remains ensured people could not act in an historical vacuum.

As the Moor continues to change, both physically and in the way it is perceived and valued, so these remains and the coherent historic landscape they comprise will continue to affect farmers and other land managers. Some remains are protected by law as nationally important monuments (Scheduled Monuments) but all the others receive an equally powerful protection, that of being valued as the legacy of former moorland individuals, families and communities. Change can almost always be planned or designed to take earlier remains into account, to avoid unnecessarily damaging old banks, walls and buildings or upsetting the historic character of the landscape.

It is hoped that this booklet helps people understand the internationally important archaeological remains on Bodmin Moor a little better so that they are respected, celebrated and enjoyed now and in the future.

The results of the various Bodmin Moor archaeological surveys (maps, plans, drawings, photographs, notes etc) are held in the offices of the Cornwall Archaeological Unit (Kennall Building, Old County Hall, Station Road, Truro, TR1 3AY; Tel 01872 323603).

Further Reading

Barnatt, J, 1982 *Prehistoric Cornwall, the Ceremonial Monuments*, Turnstone Press

Gerrard, GAM, 2000 *The Early British Tin Industry*, Tempus

Johnson, N and Rose, P, 1994 *Bodmin Moor, an archaeological survey, Volume 1, the human landscape to c1800*, English Heritage and The Royal Commission on the Historic Monuments of England.

(Volume 2, prepared by Peter Herring, Adam Sharpe, John Smith and Colum Giles, and covering post-medieval and industrial remains and landscapes, will be published in 2001)

Sharpe, A, 1993 *The Minions Survey*, Cornwall Archaeological Unit

Tilley, C, 1995 Rocks as resources: landscapes and power, *Cornish Archaeology* (journal of the Cornwall Archaeological Society), volume 34, pp 5-57

Acknowledgements

The authors and the Cornwall Archaeological Unit would like to thank Richard Walton of the Bodmin Moor Project for organising the publication of this booklet. He and Charlie David of North Cornwall District Council and Martin Eddy of Caradon District Council commented on a draft text. Mike Tippett, Steve Diment, John Brinkhoff and Dave Taylor of the Technical Services Department of Cornwall County Council's Planning Directorate prepared distribution maps and relabelled some other drawings.

We would like to thank our colleagues Rosemary Robertson, who prepared the reconstruction drawings; Steve Hartgroves, who took the aerial photographs; and Adam Sharpe, who directed the Minions Survey. Unless otherwise stated, the ground photographs were taken by the authors, Nicholas Johnson or Steve Hartgroves.